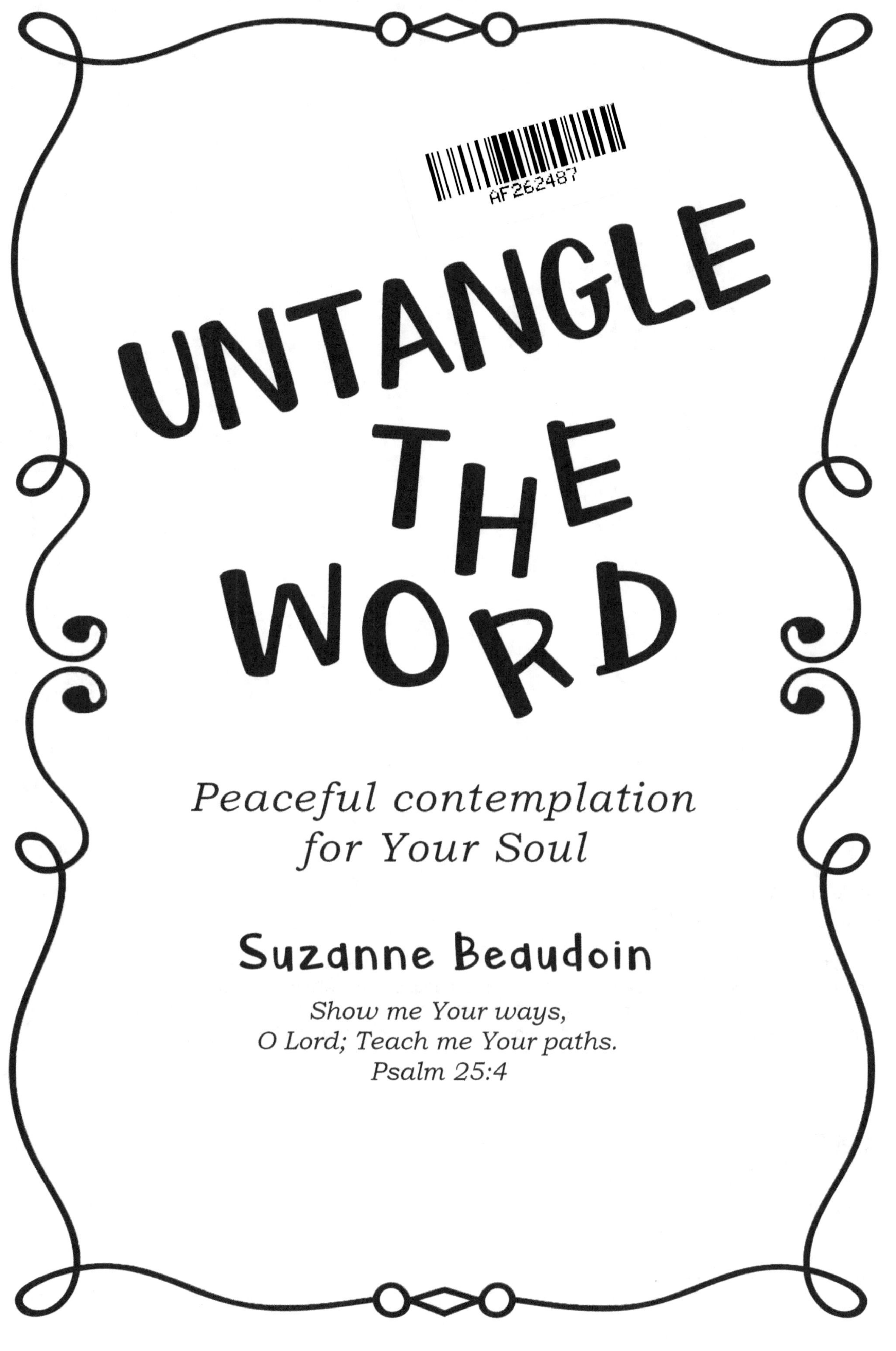

UNTANGLE THE WORD

Peaceful contemplation for Your Soul

Suzanne Beaudoin

*Show me Your ways,
O Lord; Teach me Your paths.
Psalm 25:4*

Untangle The Word
Copyright © 2019 by Suzanne Beaudoin

Tellwell Talent
www.tellwell.ca

ISBN
978-0-2288-1225-8 (Paperback)

Today we see Zentangle all over, I love the curve lines and the opportunity for any of us young and old to express our creative talent, but I also have a love for the Word of God. How nice to be able to enjoy them both at the same time.

Sharla Bruun

A dear friend of mine past away as I finished drawing this colouring book. I would like to dedicate this book to her, in memory of her love of God, and her selfless spirit May you enjoy the gift of Your Salvation. See you soon my friend

For with you is the
fountain of life;
in your light
we see light.
Psalm 36:9

for everyone who asks
receives; the one
who seeks finds; and
to the one who knocks,
the door will be
opened
Mathew 7:8
SB

faith
Hope
Love
the greatest of These is
Love
1 Cor 13:13

As for me and
my house
we will serve
the Lord
Joshua 24:15
SB

GOD
so loved the world that He gave
his one and only Son, that
whoever believe in Him
shall not perish but have
eternal life
John 3:16

12
9
3
6
There is Time for everything
and a season for every
activity under the heavens:
Ecclesiastes 3:1

Wisdom is a tree of life to those who embrace her;
happy are those who hold her tightly
Proverbs 3:18

I
HAVE
written
your
NAME
on the
PALMS
of my
HANDS
ISAIAH 49:16
SB

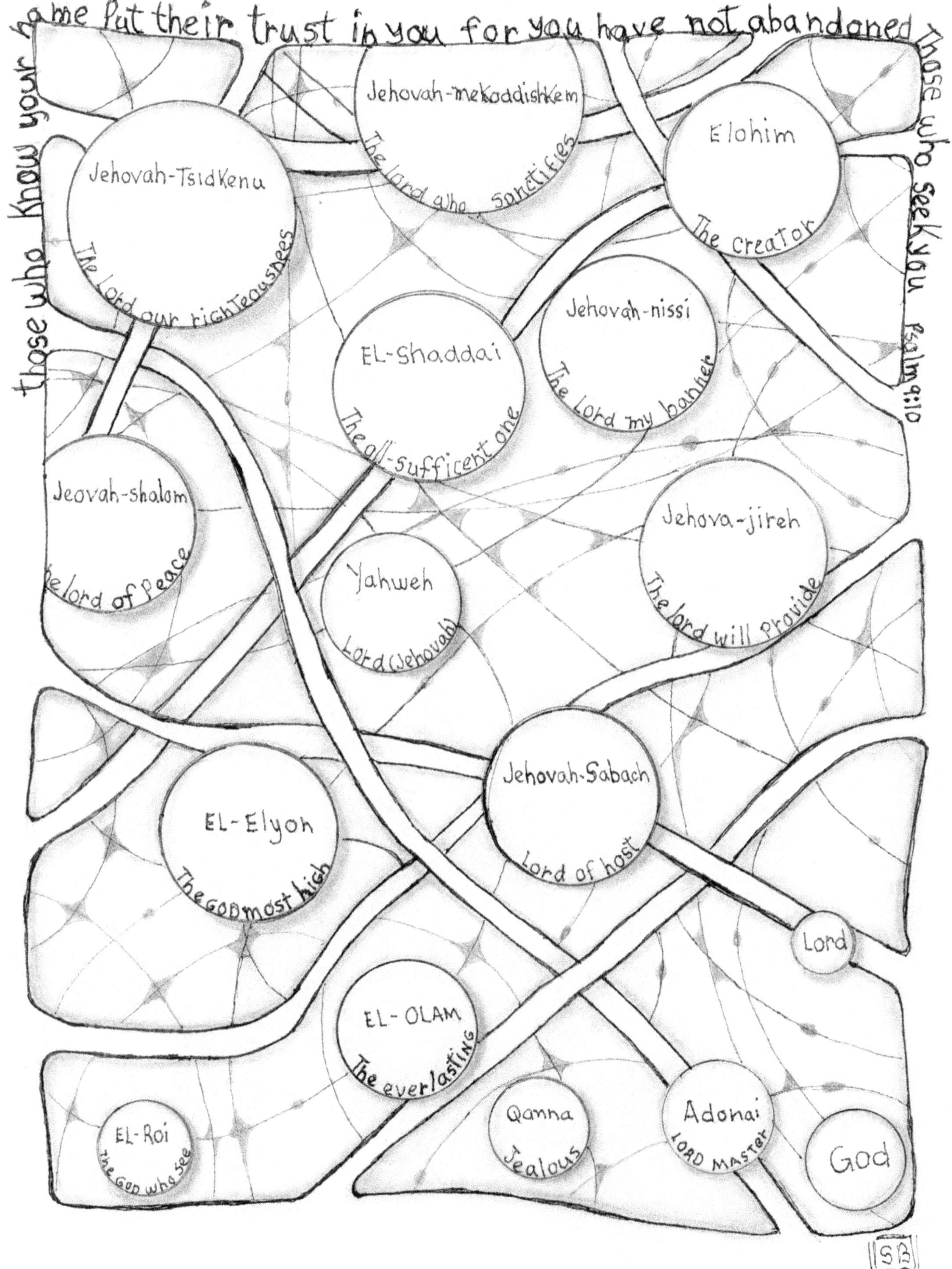

those who know your name put their trust in you for you have not abandoned those who seek you Psalm 9:10
Jehovah-Tsidkenu
The Lord our righteousness
Jehovah-mekaddishkem
The Lord who sanctifies
Elohim
The creator
El-Shaddai
The all-sufficient one
Jehovah-nissi
The Lord my banner
Jeovah-shalom
The Lord of Peace
Yahweh
Lord (Jehovah)
Jehova-jireh
The Lord will Provide
EL-Elyon
The God most high
Jehovah-Sabach
Lord of host
Lord
EL-OLAM
The everlasting
EL-Roi
The God who see
Qanna
Jealous
Adonai
Lord Master
God
SB

A man who finds wisdom
will be filled with joy
for wisdom
is more valuable
than
Silver or Gold
Proverbs 3: 13-14

She is clothed with strength
and dignity, and she
laughs with no fear of
the future
Proverbs 31:25
SB

let your light
so shine before men that
they may see your good
works and glorify your
father in Heaven
Matthew 5:16
SB

You are a love letter from Jesus
written not with ink, but with
the Spirit of the living God
2 Corinthian 3:3
SB

Lord you are more precious than Silver
Lord you are more costly than Gold
Lord you are more beautiful than
Diamonds

Then you will know the truth
and the truth will set you free.
John 8:32

Let us sing to the Lord
Let us make
Joyfull noise to the
rock of our
salvation
Ps 95:1
SB

9 780228 812258